The Future Perfect: A Fugue

Winner of the Snowbound Chapbook Award

"I am stunned, delighted, and moved by the seamless merging of meaning and music that unfolds throughout *The Future Perfect: A Fugue*. Whether made up of one sentence or a dozen, each section of this long, single work stands on its own, as self-sufficient as a painting in a museum, while contributing to the whole masterful gathering.

"This is an intricate work of decisive oscillation, of tender and careful attention shifting swiftly and precisely between the infinitesimal and the vast, and between one concrete reality and another, without ever losing its way:

> The house rages, but is not consumed. Ablaze, it stands as
> square and certain as a child's drawing. In each window:
> flames instead of curtains.

"Such sure-footed writing is astonishing. It would be an understatement to point out that the reader rarely encounters such piercing visionary states, with the author highly alert to sound and syllable, while focused on meaning:

> *Is it* disillusion *or* dissolution *that one experiences first?*

"Throughout, the author probes our capacity for perception: what do we see (the present), remember (the past), and imagine (the future)? And how do we understand them? What elevates the writing even more is the unmistakable passion and urgency pulsing throughout each of the poem's sections, the deliberate and inspired choice of every word."

—FROM THE JUDGE'S CITATION BY JOHN YAU

"The short poems in *The Future Perfect: A Fugue* trace an ambitious journey 'through the viscosity of time' from an amorphous beginning of life to a prospective end, including the lives of an individual, a species, and even a planet: 'the mountain, upheaved in an instant, erodes slowly' and 'From Europa's cracked crust, icy plumes vent. Worlds, unlimited, come into being and perish.' But it is the fine-tuned language of the in-between, its specificity and haunting familiarity, that most holds our attention and admiration:

> What matters is the miscellany, the hodgepodge, the
> mishmash, unkempt days loosely stitched to the next,
> a hinge giving in to rust, to the slow passage of rust, or
> the mind at its usual unruly industry, as noisy as gravel
> in a zinc bucket.

"The scope of the collection is epic—dance is created, the Minotaur faces the maze, stone tools disappear, Thomas the Doubter touches the wound; and ultimately the future seems one of vanishing, both for the earth and for the individual: 'the murmur of ink drying.'

"Everything is transitory; yet we watch the narrator visualize the here and now in bushes swamped in purple blossoms, a house on fire, an opaque sky, moons, pulses of rain, light in its many forms. Images appear and disappear, repeat and interweave as in a musical fugue, the impersonal voice questioning the simultaneity of what is happening, the unkempt past, memory itself. What is most moving for me is watching what the narrator calls the apparition of a body practicing presence. It is that hesitancy, that acknowledged effort— these poems."

—MARTHA RONK

Also by Eric Pankey

Not Yet Transfigured, Orison Press, 2021

Alias: Prose Poems, Free Verse Editions/Parlor Press, 2020

The Owl of Minerva, Milkweed Editions, 2019

Vestiges: Notes, Responses, & Essays, Parlor Press, 2019

Augury, Milkweed Editions, 2017

Crow-work, Milkweed Editions, 2015

Dismantling the Angel: Prose Poems, Free Verse Editions/
    Parlor Press, 2014

Trace, Milkweed Editions, 2013

The Pear as One Example: New and Selected Poems 1984-2008,
Ausable Press, 2008

Objects and Mementos (chapbook), Center for the Book Arts, 2007

Reliquaries, Ausable Press, 2005

Oracle Figures, Ausable Press, 2003

Cenotaph, Alfred A. Knopf, 2000

The Late Romances, Alfred A. Knopf, 1997

Apocrypha, Alfred A. Knopf, 1991

Heartwood, Atheneum, 1988. (reissued) Orchises, 1998

For the New Year, Atheneum, 1984

Eric Pankey, the author of many books, is Professor of English and the Heritage Chair in Writing at George Mason University. He lives with his wife, the poet Jennifer Atkinson, in Fairfax, Virginia.

Tupelo Press
P.O. Box 1767
North Adams, Massachusetts 01247
(413) 664-9611 / Fax: (413) 664-9711
editor@tupelopress.org / www.tupelopress.org

Tupelo Press is an award-winning independent literary press that publishes fine
fiction, non-fiction, and poetry in books that are a joy to hold as well as read. Tupelo
Press is a registered 501(c)(3) non-profit organization, and we rely on public support
to carry out our mission of publishing extraordinary work that may be outside the
realm of the large commercial publishers. Financial donations are welcome and are
tax deductible.

The Future Perfect: *A Fugue*

Eric Pankey

Tupelo Press
North Adams, Massachusetts

How does memory slip through the viscosity of time? How does a subfloor support the weight of trauma, an archive of dreams, a cast iron tub overflowing? With a retrospective glance, one can see clearly the narrative's broken sequence—mute bodies in motion, staggered by desire, more a dance than drama. In the scrubbed-out distance, a magpie, old emblem of confusion, calls out workbook phrases it learned in capitivity: a seductive hubbub, a sweet and oracular chatter.

Calling it a *blue distilled from dusk* does not change the fact that a shadow has no tangible content.

Wherever one walks, a cloud of gnats hovers head-high. Starlings break fast from a pear tree. Twilight lingers long above the tree line. A deer and fawn bed down beneath dark hemlocks. As the future approaches, a chained dog begins to whimper.

From an excavated meteorite, hauled up on the shingled shore, a single frequency emanates. Distance defies clarity and cannot be fixed. It withdraws. No. It encroaches. There's just enough light to reveal the dark interior of the icebergs gathered out there like the clustered notes of a chord.

How few stars to suggest the infinite?

The mountain, upheaved in an instant, erodes slowly. One watches the mountain move, watches the earth occlude the moon. Cold holds down clouds just above the tree line. The coyote's movements are tracked and mapped. Now and then a loss of signal or glitch registers as a vanishing.

As a giant in Eden, one is given the ornaments of grammar, the ornaments of wilderness. Beneath a hunter's moon, one shelters in the cave of allegory. Back then, by which one means now, everything was in the public domain: zero, for instance, and the golden ratio. One is given the whiteness of salt, the whiteness that is sky. Is it *disillusion* or *dissolution* one experiences first?

What one said returned echoed: the fog stood still; the mountain moved.

Several days into the journey, lured by the horizon's curve (and to enliven the plot), one emerges as a stowaway. At what depth will the light not penetrate? Bewitched, the compass needle points it one direction.

In the wake of marks and traces, how to itemize the pandemonium? How to accommodate the allusion without a source—the washed-out silk of mirage, the wash on the line—and not botch the figures and sums? To say *gesture* is to evoke a body involved in the making. Has the dance begun before the dancers move?

Sometimes one's convinced one's seen a ghost. One feels faint and for a moment vision blurs. A bit of gold leaf snagged on an acacia shimmers at a high frequency in the breeze. Such quickened enthusiasms! Such transport! The dizzying quiver and flux soon pass. The search is never for fire—all motion and efficiency—but for a contraption impregnated by light.

What matters is the miscellany, the hodgepodge, the mishmash, unkempt days loosely stitched to the next, a hinge giving in to rust, to the slow passage of rust, or the mind at its usual unruly industry, as noisy as gravel in a zinc bucket, a medley, a potpourri, a salmagundi, the moon mistaken for a blossom in a mistaken translation of a Chinese poem, the mélange, the welter, the motley muddle, the train as it approaches the station trailing smoke—an amalgam of combustible cinders, an alloy of smudge and ash. One could lose sleep making sense of the grab bag of all the *this* and the *that*, the hash, the rehash, the leftovers, the gumbo a different recipe in each spoonful. Like it or not, the sundries accumulate: a collection without taxonomy, a torn crazy quilt, a ragbag of hand-me-downs.

On the garden's raised beds, the moon is a white scab of salt. If only experience were immediate, which is to say, unmediated. A single slug scales a cabbage stalk. In the distance: an inscrutable verge, so far away it remains to be seen.

Stone tools outlive their usefulness. Voids and solids, reconfigured, are called a room, a house, an interior. Memories gather there as residue, as dust. Duration suggests a beginning and end, yet there is no recollection of birth or death. For now: these notes, these intervals.

Beyond: blunted peaks, cloud-girdled. The air rare, white as limestone, vivid. Two trees endure in the old orchard. Like a contraption in a disappearing act, a cloth-covered birdcage hangs by a wire. Appearances, noted in the present, occur like all things light-revealed, lit by the past.

The sky and sea are drab, grainy: a long passage of sleep without dreams, without underpinnings or a lacework of roots. Does one affix the memory of tides to some tidal memory, without a middle distance to distinguish the *near* from the *far*, the idea of *north* from *true north* itself?

From Europa's cracked crust, icy plumes vent. Worlds, unlimited, come into being and perish. While planting an olive tree, a treasure is uncovered. Salt is angular, twisted; bitter is asymmetrical, smooth. Amber attracts chaff as a lodestone draws iron fillings. Is stasis or motion a proper attribute of the soul? Iron is, consequently, hard. And lead is heavy.

The sky—taut, silken—is stripped back with turpentine, blurred by time. The path is a scar. Each mark conceals a belabored query. A barricade of tires burns at the border. Slung rocks plummet like sudden hail.

How not to project into the future, not to see the past as portent? Light exposes the image. Exposed to light, the image begins to disintegrate.

The owl is not an oracle, nor the sparrow a scintilla of God's attention. Each room in the apiary is hexagonal, overfull with viscous ooze. How soon before the last colony collapses?

One arrives with an invitation of ether and stars. One arrives exhausted. One arrives to a fanfare, to the erasures of amnesia. One arrives with a preexisting condition, although the symptoms mask themselves. In the grip of pleasure, one arrives. What of the narrative can a single frame hold? A closed door? As always, the concurrent must be conveyed in sequence. A door opens onto a frayed fog-edge, onto an eroded boundary, onto a shadow-cast of lilacs. The past, scuttled, is still visible beneath the surface. Look: a pool of glacial melt, light from the north, the dusk's blue palette. By recognizing objects in photographs one proves again one is not a robot.

What is that bush called, swamped in purple blossoms, a ragged notation gone wild, at once threshold and passage? In rough wind, it's a pentimento of reconsidered brushstrokes.

Between figure and ground, a stage is set for the viewer. The parallel plots, being parallel, never waver nor intersect. And watching, reckoning with time, one feels, not exiled, but displaced, surrounded by the dredged-up and extraneous, fodder and ciphers. One attempts to forget the others seated beside, behind, or in front, to forget that the common experience of the darkened theater, the individual threads woven to make up the snow-blind blank space of the screen. Up close, one notices more and more subatomic particles fill in the void: blips and specks, a blurred dirty white tundra. Soon one forgets one is reading the subtitles as they appear, seven to nine syllables at a time, and one is fluent in Greek or Hungarian, or some indigenous and endangered language about to slip from usage. As an actor speaks one feels one's own tongue touch the back of one's front teeth, one's mouth opens around the air of a vowel. An o, perhaps. It is as though one has awakened in the night of a sleeping car to a single word spoken out of a dream clearly, directly. And in that word: a thousand miles crossed, one tie after another, the gravel bed's angle of repose shimmered, shuddered. At last undermined.

Beneath the thin overlay of time, one can observe the infinite distances between two adjacent points, the slow growth of spores, the stalactite's irregular drip, even minute particles of pigment diffuse in a wash of mineral spirits.

The angel—a lens in images of the Annunciation—focuses to a pinpoint the projection, but leaves no mark, no record of *having-been-there*.

The past carded and spun makes a coarse thread good for rough stitches. Or tying up tomato vines. One has a ladder, but nothing to lean it against. One skirts the issue; one glimpses a slip. Boredom is a given in purgatory, as it is here.

The story gets the better of the teller. Incongruous memories surface: unwilled, untitled. The obscure synopsis should have clued one in. One renames one's doubts *ambivalence*.

One cuts open a hailstone and finds a crystal lattice, a bit of grit. One looks in vain for the imperfect stitch that confirms at last *handmadeness*.

A truce is always fragile, as when the board of directors questions the lasting value and aesthetic merit of the recent acquisitions. One's deliberate delays do not counter impermanence, do not make visible that which otherwise remains hidden.

In an old field recording of a chain gang's work song, the sledgehammers come down not quite in unison. The gang keeps time as well as it can be kept.

Smoke enters the room and one crawls to the fire assembly point, is accounted for, remains a safe distance from the building. One is drawn to symmetry and at home in melancholia. One cannot hear the river's sidewinding, cannot hear the rain's white noise above the fire's racket.

One complains about the weight and burden of the mask, but, in fact, the mask is made of a fine silk lace and stitched rags of wasp paper. One walks face-first into a spider's web. When a snare slips, one is entangled in a bowerbird's lair, in a prickly rose.

Beyond the window, intervals of blue in the middle distance lend substance to light, light to substance. In the interior space—infiltrated, light-suffused—the apparition of the body itself practices presence, the improbable possibilities of visibility.

Cigarette smoke enters from off-screen. In the previous scene, someone enters the sanctum of the woods and is forbidden to gather fallen branches from the forest floor, to build a fire. The fallen snow seems a plaster cast of another, forgotten world. On the soundtrack, the pricks and glimmers of bell tones. A slow, childlike tune plucked on a cello.

One could foresee the potential calamity ahead on the unfinished dance floor, but for some reason one held one's tongue and, as one anticipated, the bodies tumbled and eventually, amid the screams, the music stopped. One is encouraged to shelter in place, to make due, to hold tight. One predicts the predicament but is encouraged again not to rush in to anything.

The template allows one to draw every imaginable floor plan that might be pieced together from the modular units, but none seems habitable: a space one might experience as a *duration*. The stock photos hung on the wall do not help, nor the books arranged by jacket cover color, moving from cool blues to the warmest reds. One signs the lease nonetheless. Moves in.

One enters the quarantine of sleep willfully, sketches in night with a charred willow branch, with a pigment of burnt bone. One sets a trap for the moon, stretches out a parachute to collect condensation. Night eschews a chronological ordering, thus one is truant within the moment. Not *constellation*, one thinks, but *asterism*. Not a *fetish* but a *tomato-shaped pincushion*.

Hourly, the pathway reconfigures itself. The Minotaur's choices seem few: right, left, straight ahead, or backtrack. The labyrinth is an architecture of elaborate and abstruse logic. Logic does not comfort, but confines. If the Minotaur charges and gores a wall, the wall repairs itself. He is not cursed, but is, if truth be told, too dull-headed to learn that with a reasoned thought or two the maze will unfold itself before him into the shortest distance between two points; that he needs only to lift the heavy bull mask from his human face to find an exit sign.

Ice reflects an opaque sky. As it moves through a stand of firs, the wind slips up and down its octave. Clouds scud. The day moon remains—an abrasion on glass, a nail-scratched locket, a coin defaced, a glacial basin burnished onto the firmament. Navigable inland waterways freeze. Birds fall from flight. Great swathes of forests are felled. Crops fail. Famine. Bodies unburied breed plagues and poxes. How does one avoid thinking about the *void?* One burns witches, who manipulate and control the weather; one spends what precious fuel is left.

One is as restless as one who approaches an ending; as calm as one can be in the quiet moment before a soliloquy begins. A sudden instant of hailstones clatters in a boat's hull. A broken stoneware jar hangs in a tree for a bird to nest in.

In the attic, haunted by a single wasp, the turbine fan cannot disperse the heat that joists, insulation, and plywood frame in. The stacked boxes—old photos and tax files—wait as kindling for the serenade of a spark. The combustion is spontaneous; fire gives birth to fire. One stands, unscathed, at a distance from the house, and beholds the fire, the garish spectacle of its robes. The house rages, but is not consumed. Ablaze, it stands as square and certain as a child's drawing of a house. In each window: flames instead of curtains.

A king awaits a cargo of gold, ivory, pearls, and sandalwood from Ophir. Before the treasure arrives a forest reclaims the palace. The forest is a garden: intimately scaled, and adhering to a sacred geometry. Rejoice. As the seeker advances, God recedes. This is the origin of dance.

Along the prairie flyway, what kerning and leading holds the flock together? Each bird apart?

The confluence of the rivers is set down as a calligraphic abstraction. A dark reservoir without reflection, the floodplain stretches to the horizon. Which is more: *as little as possible*? Or *as much as is necessary*? Or is the question: *which is less*?

Winter ends with a miscellany's logic: a leaden horizon, a narrow but unbridgeable distance. Stolen moments are exchanged for isolated hours, elaborate entanglements, lodging. One's suitable room fulfills a double assignment as a stage and shelter. The heady pollen of stargazer lilies covers the bureaus, the desktop, and end tables. Beyond the window, the sacred mountain is depleted of snow. On a frequency at the far end of the dial, one can hear vespers, and recalls the little Latin one learned long ago, knowing even then it would come in handy.

Thomas the Doubter enters the wound as one might a cave. To exit, as from a womb, is the difficult part.

One wants not just efficiency, but a simple design as well, the way an old ballad stores an exact dose of sadness, the way a bloom of jellyfish disappears into the murk. Each problem solved, dissolves. By all accounts a hedgerow absorbs the traffic noise. How many seasons has the ladder leaned against the gutter? Far north and further afield, one kneels like a pilgrim. The canvas, roughly stitched together, keeps the sleet out. One adjusts the perpetual motion machine's flywheel between a pair of heavy magnets. Set in motion, the contraption keeps going, and because it keeps going one figures it will continue.

Memory is after all a mode of abstraction, a navigational marker anchored in endlessness. Given the state one's in, one just might try to chart and map a flock of evening chimney swifts, might carry a candlestick across a distance to illuminate not the *invisible*, but the *unviable*. What is the provenance of that skull at the foot of the cross? Why does one find one's self so often waylaid in a disquieting tableau?

A mirror cannot fix the fleeting, cannot conjoin temporalities in complex narratives. Although one stands ruthlessly naked before it, the mirror sees as if for the first time. Assisted by another mirror, a mirror performs the trick of infinite repetitions. Constructs a corridor of receding echoes. Call it *image apparatus* or *looking glass*, its only art is mimicry.

Today is a series of small interventions—neither fugue, nor aftermath—a hedge, perhaps, against some future loss. The ordinary is preordained, even as a slight shift in scale emerges preserved in the *now*. The room itself, a façade, before which a drama has unfolded, is scrubbed of context, of isolated gestures, as if, having never seen the movie, one recalled an isolated film still, the way shadow fell so that no single face is illuminated. Whatever *has been* or is *about to be* is lit poorly. Nonetheless, one has moved on, even as the empire declines into ruin and the bones of giants are exhumed. *Nonetheless*, one says, getting little traction.

To resolve the apparent discord of two notes, in an empty room with piano, a third note is sounded. Longing pervades. One understands this, as one understands the frail luster of afternoon light on a plum—

neither red nor purple—but oddly buttery. How to narrate desire as more than ache? As less than narrative? After the first two, the third note slips from hearing.

A photograph of a windswept arctic expanse entitled *A Sublime & Icy Prospect*. A coat stitched from nettles. The sensation of a tongue pressed against a loosened tooth. Wax cylinder recordings of soliloquies. Scrap silver. A peripheral drift. The reservoir of a notebook. The archive as a point of departure. A Florentine window above Santo Spirito. An instance of clairvoyance dismissed.

A retinue of sleepwalkers gains the other shore. Soon they will open doors, which open onto doors, which open onto doors. One waits on the other side: one's passport still in the customs agent's hand, still under the custom agent's scrutiny, unstamped.

Overnight, a circle of mushrooms appears: black-gilled, their caps pocked, frog-belly white, their annuli torn—ragged foreskins— abominable, obscene, ill-omened.

A note from a flute of elder wood. A fabricated diary. The water a boat displaces. The future as a place of exile. The photograph as a caesura between *before* and *after*. The grid and its austere function. The *m* that distinguishes a *comma* from a *coma*. Alluvial marshlands. The borrowing of one's enemy's arrows. The object rehabilitated through reuse. Incidental objects on a minor planet. A dark chamber fitted with a lens. An exemplar liberated from rebirth. The murmur of ink drying.

On either side of the street, the dogs long ago settled their territorial dispute. No one dances these days upon the worn floorboards of the union hall. Next door a young woman fastens a necklace of seed pearls, recalls the fragile wingspan of her mother's collarbones. From a throng of sleet, the caretaker emerges and jiggles a wrong key in the lock. When one dog barks, the other starts as per the conditions of their treaty.

The soul, seeking sweetness, departs the body as a bee, delineates from the chaos a path among black-eyed susans, alighting here and there on the surface tension of time, teetering as wind intervenes in the grasses and treetops. A memory reiterated becomes a *new*, an *other* memory, and whatever has been accentuated or occluded is no less real. The subject, of course, is the simultaneity of *what happened*, the narrative inferred by what the eavesdropper misheard, the elisions and incongruities smoothed out, but the clutter undistilled. It is not surprising the attention the barely discernable receives, the gaps and exclusions in the pulse of rain, for instance, or the erasures, which, upon a second look, are quite evident. The soul—there must be a rational explanation—comes and goes at will, possesses a lucid and somber solidity. Today: a bee. Tomorrow: a lizard or perhaps a little armored pill bug (the only crustacean, by the way, fully adapted to life on land). It is essential to narrow one's subject, but the digressions pile up like loess, shift and collapse as one attempts to walk away.

The screen flares then settles into its grayish white. The film, snapped, clacks against the reel.

One stands at last in front of the house the locals call *The House of the Hanged Man*. Having come a long way, one senses beyond the tree line some force or foreboding. There is no record of the hanged man or of a hanging in the town archives. No doubt there is an explanation. One enters without knocking, as is the custom, and calls out. No one answers. Ravels of threads stand in as curtains. A toppled ladder-back chair occupies the dining room, but no rope hangs from the exposed rafters, which slump beneath the roof's ongoing collapse. A little rain (it's started to rain since one entered) falls on the stone floor. From the unshuttered windows, one takes in the upward slope, the restrained palette of the medieval hilltop town. Is it possible to enter uninvited and remain politely distant? So as not to be provocative, thunder waits until one has forgotten the presence of lightning to sound, and the rain, like a clock, ticks on the stone casements. In the valley, perhaps, wolves disrupt the foxhunt. The mown hay molders in the fields. The day, just about to pivot to evening, shines like a polished stone, something one might pick up on a path and pocket, only to find later while doing the wash and wonder why this stone and not another? One sets the stone upon a sill, nonetheless: a keepsake kept after all, like the name of this house for its namesake.

Not the gloaming or the interface of first light, but the point in one's movement called here.

Jesus, the wounded healer, descends a steep stairwell to the realm of the dead. Sometimes night comes, but the edges don't meet. Sometimes it's dark enough to see stars. Jesus has yet to learn patience, the theological difference between *both* and *either or.* A precarious light, he crosses a vast distance. A linga of flame, he flares but nothing catches. The dead, by reflex, turn away from his scalded flesh.

A flame's pneumatic body. The charred spent tip of a match. A house without mirrors. Multiple readings of the empty space. To say *There is nothing I want. Nothing at all.* An arrested motion. An apnea. The drama of scale. The surface pearlescent. The currents awry. An exhumed ship's hull marl-blackened, skeletal. A world sung into being. The equity of light and shadow. To say *I wanted for nothing, but wanted nonetheless.*

The story so far is all rehearsal, what one calls *standard procedure,* and no date set for the performance. To add edge to uncertainty, the problem is a problem of vigilance and one is down to a skeleton crew. One admits one is an emptied skiff, a placeholder, a null field. To recognize the invisible, one approximates the infinite. It's total immersion or nothing.

Far fewer days ahead than behind. And each set down in parallel graphite lines. Although ruled, errors and random interference interrupt the parallel, give the graph the look of lake water after a breeze has passed, of ripples diminishing at an almost steady rate. One recalls now one almost drowned in this lake in 1966. Above: clouds cut from jade. Clouds uprooted.

Fog is the weft; fog is the warp: a weave without visible increments. The boat's wake arrives before the boat. The argument is tangled, tangential. A spun thread is drawn long, the curve of its slack calculable. In a Venetian ambrotype, the dome's oculus returns God's gaze.

One longs to align the elements, to disrupt invisibility, but only the ancillary emerges in moonlight. The hills and mesas inscribed by rain and wind are like scrolls and codices. How vast forgetting becomes. One looks up and finds a momentary map of meteors, a thread not yet entirely severed. One turns to cosmology, numerology, mysticism, and analysis to disinter the past, when a shovel would do the trick. Wind's tremolo through cottonwoods documents distance. The moon, held down by a jagged line of solder, does not set. What can be unearthed by way of a long exposure? One lives in the rain shadow. An unkempt edge delineates the property line: a little wilderness to keep others out. One is guilty often of the trespass of a gaze, yet whatever is seen is partial: a diffuse reflection in an isolated body of water, for instance. How does one, as Willa Cather suggests, *imprison for a moment the shining*? The first intent was to catch fire, then to release it.

What if one spoke only in the future perfect? What if, as it leapt, the tiger atomized into a swarm of bees? What if the day-before-yesterday did not hover in the blind spot, a schism between abstraction and figuration? What if one refused to watch the effigies torn apart, resewn, and torn apart again?

Acknowledgments

ARKANSAS INTERNATIONAL:
The Future Perfect [A note from a]

AMERICAN JOURNAL OF POETRY:
The Future Perfect [In the wake of]
The Future Perfect [What is that bush]
The Future Perfect [The angel–a lens]
The Future Perfect [The story gets the]
The Future Perfect [One cuts open a]
The Future Perfect [In an old field]
The Future Perfect [Beneath the thin overlay]
The Future Perfect [Smoke enters the room]
The Future Perfect [One complains about the]
The Future Perfect [A truce is always]
The Future Perfect [The past carded and]
The Future Perfect [What if one spoke]
The Future Perfect [Cigarette smoke enters from]
The Future Perfect [One could foresee the]
The Future Perfect [The template allows one]
The Future Perfect [One enters the quarantine]
The Future Perfect [The flame's pneumatic body]

AMERICAN LIFE IN POETRY:
The Future Perfect [Winter ends with a]

DIODE:

The Future Perfect [A giant in Eden, one]
The Future Perfect [Several days into the]
The Future Perfect [Sometimes one's convinced one's]

GEORGIA REVIEW:

The Future Perfect [Winter ends with a]

GETTYSBURG REVIEW:

The Future Perfect [On either side of]
The Future Perfect [What matters is the]

GRIS-GRIS:

The Future Perfect [Wherever ones walks, a]

NATURAL BRIDGE:

The Future Perfect [Overnight, a circle of]

NEW WORLD WRITING:

The Future Perfect [What one said returned]

PHANTOM DRIFT:

The Future Perfect [Hourly, the pathway reconfigures]
The Future Perfect [Ice reflects an opaque]

POETRY INTERNTIONAL:

The Future Perfect [The soul, seeking sweetness]
The Future Perfect [Jesus, the wounded healer]

SOUTHERN POETRY REVIEW:

The Future Perfect [How few stars does]
The Future Perfect [The mountain, upheaved in]

TALKING RIVER:

The Future Perfect [On the garden's raised]
The Future Perfect [Stone tools outlive their]
The Future Perfect [Beyond: blunted peaks, cloud-girdled]
The Future Perfect [The sky and sea are]
The Future Perfect [From Europa's cracked crust]
The Future Perfect [The sky—taut, silken]
The Future Perfect [How not to project]
The Future Perfect [The owls are not]

TERRAIN:

The Future Perfect [Calling it a blue]

Recent and Selected Titles from Tupelo Press